Contents

Copyright Notice

This book is dedicated
to the woman I was in 2003
trying so hard to be loved,
trying so hard to be enough,
and not even knowing who she really was.
I see you now!

Introduction

Why I Wrote This Book

I wrote this book because I got tired of watching strong women lie to themselves.

Yes, lie.

"I don't need anyone."
"I'm just unlucky in love."
"All the good men are taken."
"I just attract broken ones."

No.

You attract what your energy is aligned with.

And if you keep ending up in the same dynamic with a different face, it's not coincidence. It's a pattern.

For over a decade in the dating and coaching world, I sat across from thousands of clients. Brilliant women. Accomplished women. Women who could run companies, raise children, survive divorce, rebuild from nothing.

And still... crumble the moment they met someone they actually liked.

Overthinking every text.
Giving too much too fast.
Trying to control the outcome.
Calling it intuition when it was really fear.

Different stories. Same wiring.

And I know this not just because I coached it but because I lived it.

My own dark night of the soul cracked me open. It forced me to see that I was the common denominator in every relationship I had ever been in. That realization stung.

But it was also the most empowering moment of my life.

Because if I was the common denominator, I could change the equation.

In a moment of total collapse, I had no choice but to surrender to something outside myself. I looked to the sky, screamed out for help "Someone please help me!" and in a millisecond it led to something I can't logically explain, a moment of complete release where unconditional love flooded my system and calmed everything. My tears. My racing thoughts. My nervous system.

I call it Nirvana. It was a love, a feeling I had never felt before.

That experience changed everything.

It awakened a deeper inner knowing. A connection to guidance beyond the logical mind. The kind of insight that doesn't come from a book, it comes through you

And after that, I needed to understand what had just happened.

That's what led me into energy work. Into trauma work. Into studying emotional patterns, childhood imprints, survival responses, and how they shape who we choose and what we tolerate. Ultimately what was that energy that enveloped my body and gave me such a feeling of peace.

Here's what I've learned:

You don't attract partners.
You attract reflections.

If you are still operating from shame, fear of abandonment, control, guilt, or the need to prove, you will recreate that dynamic over and over again.

Not because you're broken.

Because you're unconscious of the subconscious patterns.

That's the hard truth.

This book is a parable made from years of watching these patterns unfold. It's woven from real clients, real breakdowns, real breakthroughs, and my own.

I wrote it because people don't need more dating advice.

They need a reality shift.

And reality only shifts when you do.

How to Use This Book

If you read this straight through without stopping, you're wasting your time.

The chapters are short on purpose. The discomfort is intentional.

The journal prompts are not optional. They are the work.

This is not about understanding the character in the story.

It's about recognizing yourself in it.

When something stings… pause.

When something makes you defensive… write.

When something makes you want to skip ahead… slow down.

You don't need to relive every painful memory from your past. But you do need to see what you're still dragging into your present relationships.

If you want a partner who sees you fully, drop the performance.

If you want to be chosen, stop auditioning.

If you want real love, stop operating from fear.

And yes, that requires inner work.

The kind where you stop blaming.
Stop waiting.
Stop pretending you don't care.

Do this book slowly. Honestly. Privately.

If you do, you will feel a shift before the final page.

Not because I wrote something clever.

Because you finally stopped running from yourself.

About the Author

Deborah Knight is a straight-talking spiritual alchemist, coach, speaker, and author known for her no-fluff, straight-to-the-heart approach to transformation.

Her path into this work began with heartbreak. What started as personal healing became a deeper inquiry into why strong, capable women so often end up carrying everything alone, in life and in love.

That question became her life's work.

Since 2006, Deborah has worked at the intersection of emotional healing, energetic alignment, and relationship dynamics. Trained through Coaches Training Institute (CTI) and certified in multiple healing modalities: including Full Spectrum Healing, Innerwise, Bio-Well energy scanning, Magnified Healing, Divine Dharma Meditation, NLP, and NCI. She blends trauma-informed awareness with energetic recalibration.

For over a decade, she worked in the dating and matchmaking world as both Matchmaker and Relationship Coach, sitting across from thousands of clients. Different backgrounds. Different trauma. Same emotional loops. The same longing for love.

Along the way, Deborah learned to trust her instinct, the quiet clarity beneath fear and conditioning. What some call intuition, she understands as attunement: a connection to something greater that guides perception, timing, and choice. That inner guidance has been instrumental in both her own healing and the breakthroughs of the people she serves.

Her volunteer service spans more than 30 years, mentoring teen mothers, working the overnight hotline for abused women at Bridges in New Hampshire, and speaking monthly inside the women's ward at Middlesex County Jail. These experiences sharpened her understanding of resilience, accountability, and the human capacity for change.

Deborah's work is forward-focused. She teaches people how to clear emotional patterns stored in the body, reset their energy, and stop recreating old stories in new relationships. When you change what you carry internally, what responds externally changes. Not by force. By who you've become..

She is the founder of the Future You Now mentorship, her signature program designed to help individuals step into the version of themselves who no longer operates from survival, but from clarity, self-trust, and conscious creation.

Deborah believes we are not meant to do life alone. When a woman heals and steps into aligned partnership, she doesn't just change her life, she elevates what's possible for everyone around her.

Her life reflects the work she teaches.

PROLOGUE

I Miss Myself

Journal Entry – Tuesday, 7:46 p.m.
Rain hitting the window like it had something to say.

It wasn't some dramatic breakdown. No rock bottom. No screaming in the shower or sobbing on the bathroom floor.

It was my reflection.

Just me. In the mirror. After another long, forgettable day.
No music. No makeup. No masks.
Just eyes that used to light up when I talked about life.
Eyes that used to sparkle with ideas, with hunger, with soul.

But tonight? Empty.
Like a house no one's lived in for years, still beautiful, but hollow as hell.

I stared at that woman, same skin, same hair, same damn body but she didn't look like me.
She looked like someone who'd been going through the motions for a long time.
She looked tired. Like... soul-tired.

And the truth hit me hard:
I miss who I was, I miss myself.

I miss the woman who *felt* everything.
Who laughed loud and cried hard and didn't apologize for either.
Who wrote like her life depended on it and danced barefoot in the kitchen because she felt free not because it looked good on a damn Instagram reel.

I used to chase sunsets.
I used to stop mid-walk just to smell jasmine in bloom and let it wreck me with beauty.
Now? I barely notice.

Between raising two incredible kids, building a business from nothing, and trying to look like the woman who has it all together. I disappeared.
Bit by bit. Smile by smile. Until I became a highlight reel instead of a human.

Polished. Poised. Pretending.

The world saw strength.
But what they didn't see?
The invisible cracks.
The numbness under the mask of perfection.
The exhaustion buried under the smile and "I'm fine."

It didn't happen all at once. It never does.
It was slow. Quiet. Like a thief stealing pieces of me while I was busy being everything to everyone else.

And tonight, for the first time, I couldn't unsee it.
That bathroom mirror held up a truth I've been dodging for years.

I've been living like a ghost.
Showing up. Smiling. Crushing goals.
But inside?
A void I could no longer ignore.

After a day full of empty meetings and fake smiles, I stopped at the store, drove home, and just... sat.
In the driveway.
Groceries in the backseat.
Engine off.
Rain falling.
And I felt... nothing.
Not even enough energy to cry.

That's when it hit me, **I can't live like this anymore.**

I can't keep pretending that this picture-perfect life is enough.
I can't keep showing up for everyone but myself.

I can't keep silencing the woman inside me who's screaming to be seen, felt, heard.

I don't have the answers yet. I don't have the roadmap.
But tonight, I felt something flicker.
A spark.
A pulse.
The tiniest echo of the woman I used to be.

Maybe the comeback doesn't start with a plan.
Maybe it starts with a whisper.
A quiet reckoning.
A gut-level confession:

I miss myself.

That's where I am right now.
Not at rock bottom. Not broken.
But standing in the quiet wreckage of a life that looks good from the outside and feels hollow on the inside.

And from this place, raw, real, stripped down, I'm ready.
Not for another performance.
Not for another damn role.
But for the *truth*.

I'm coming home to me. The hell with pleasing and taking care of everyone else,

And this time, I'm not apologizing for the spark I bring with me

CHAPTER ONE

Ghost in the Mirror

You know that moment when you stop long enough to realize you don't recognize your own damn life? That was me.

I wasn't falling apart in some dramatic way, no visible breakdown, no screaming, no shattering dishes. But inside? I was gone. Just a shell walking through the motions. A high-functioning, over-performing ghost.

Sure, on paper everything looked fine. More than fine. Two amazing kids. A business that was thriving. Smiles on cue. Clean house. Polished life. But the truth? I was disappearing behind it all.

It starts so subtly. You say yes when you mean no. You smile when you want to scream. You push your feelings down because, honestly, who has time for a breakdown when there are bills to pay, lunches to pack, clients to serve, and a hundred other things you're expected to do flawlessly?

I was the woman everyone came to for advice, for comfort, for strength. And I gave it, every damn time. Until one day, I woke up and realized I had nothing left to give myself.

That's when the mirror started telling the truth.

I'd catch glimpses of myself in store windows or bathroom reflections and think: *Who is that woman? When did her fire go out?*

I used to be wild and curious and full of heart. I used to believe in magic, real, soul-deep, universe-has-my-back magic. I used to dance, create, and cry without shame. I used to feel alive. Now those moments are few and far between.

Now? I was efficient. Controlled. Numb.

And I know I'm not alone. Maybe you're reading this with tears in your eyes because something in you knows exactly what I'm talking about. Maybe you've spent years being what everyone needed you to be, and you're exhausted from holding it all together. Or maybe you're like I was, high-achieving and successful, but completely disconnected from your inner light.

This isn't just about burnout. It's about betrayal, the kind we do to ourselves when we abandon who we are in order to be accepted, praised, or simply survive.

But here's the thing: your soul doesn't go quietly. It whispers. It nudges. And eventually, it demands to be heard.

Mine did.

That ghost in the mirror? She wasn't dead. She was dormant. Waiting for me to remember. Waiting for me to reclaim the woman I'd buried under the weight of obligation, expectation and perfectionism.

And here's what I've learned: the path back to yourself isn't neat or polite. It's messy. It's sacred. And it's necessary.

Because the world doesn't need more perfect women.
It needs more *real* ones.
More women who rise not because they're unshaken,
but because they're done being invisible.

Your Turn:

When was the last time you looked at your life and thought, 'Where the hell did I go?' Write about the moment you realized you've been running on autopilot, and what you miss most about that version of you!

Then ask: If I called that part of me back today, what energy or experience would I begin to magnetize into my life? How would my life look different?

CHAPTER TWO

Polished Surface, Shattered Inside

On the outside, I looked like I had it all dialed in. Polished, composed, successful. The kind of woman who could juggle clients, kids, deadlines, and dinner without breaking a sweat. People saw me and assumed I was solid, stable, grounded, unshakeable and I was.

However deep within me...

Deep inside?

Cracked. Crushed under the weight of expectations. Held together by nothing more than muscle memory and a to-do list.

And the most exhausting part? The act.

It wasn't just society I was performing for. It was the man I loved, too. Or at least the version of him I thought I needed to please. I slowly morphed into the woman I thought he wanted. Calmer. Softer. Less opinionated. More agreeable. I swallowed my truth to keep the peace. Played small to avoid conflict. Bit my tongue more times than I can count just to hold it all together.

I became so good at the role, I forgot it was a role.

Until the relationship broke and I was left standing in the wreckage, trying to figure out what I did wrong. What could I have done differently? Then it dawned on me, the true version of me had left the relationship long before.

That's the thing about shape-shifting in relationships. You become so fluid, so adaptable, that you don't even notice you're disappearing. You tell yourself, it's compromise. Maturity. Love. But it's really self-abandonment dressed up in politeness and when it ends, when the illusion finally collapses, you're not just grieving the relationship. You're grieving the parts of yourself you silenced to make it work.

What Is Disconnected Self Syndrome™?

Disconnected Self Syndrome™ happens when you've slowly abandoned your true self to meet expectations, avoid conflict, or keep the peace. It doesn't happen in one big moment — it creeps in through small compromises:

- Saying yes when you mean no.
- Silencing your needs to make others comfortable.
- Performing strength when you're exhausted inside.
- Trading authenticity for approval.

On the outside, you look fine, successful, dependable, even thriving. But on the inside, you feel numb, invisible, and hollow, like you're living someone else's life. You have moments of happiness however that deep sense of connection and joy have been missing for a long time.

The good news? What's disconnected can be reconnected. Your soul is never gone — it's waiting for you to come back home.

I remember staring at myself in the mirror not long after that breakup and thinking, *Damn. You've been lying to yourself for years.*

And it wasn't just about him. It was about every time I told myself "It's fine" when it wasn't. Every time I let someone's comfort matter more than my truth. Every time I smiled through pain. Every time I chose peace over honesty.

That slow erasure of self? That's what creates the disconnect.

You can only numb yourself for so long before your soul starts to raise hell. And mine did. Through anxiety. Fatigue. Apathy. Restlessness. That sense that something's wrong, even when you can't quite name what it is.

I didn't need a new hobby or a vacation. I needed to remember who the hell I was before I became everything to everyone else.

I needed to peel off the layers of performative perfection and get real.

Because here's the truth: looking like you've got it together isn't the same as being whole and fulfilled on a soul level.

When your life becomes more about how it looks than how it *feels*, you're living someone else's version of success.

This chapter of my life? It was the wake-up call. Not a gentle nudge. A full-body jolt. The universe is saying: *It's time!*

Time to stop hiding. Time to stop molding. Time to stop shrinking.

Because the version of me I buried to keep things running smoothly, she was the real one and she was done being silent, and invisible to herself and done being everyone's happy.

Your Turn

Where have you compromised yourself? When have you shut down for fear of disrupting the peace?

Where have you silently erased your 'yes' in the past week just to keep the peace?

CHAPTER THREE

The Illusion of Connection

You can have a thousand friends, a picture-perfect partner, and still feel completely alone.

That's the thing nobody warns you about. Loneliness doesn't always look like solitude. Sometimes, it looks like a full calendar. Sometimes, it looks like a shared bed and dead silence. Sometimes, it looks like smiling at the dinner table while your soul is starving.

I was surrounded by people. Family. Clients. Neighbors. A man who claimed to love me. And yet, I felt like I was fading. Not because they didn't care. But because I was nowhere in the equation.

People said I was "so easy to talk to." That I was "always there for them." I wore that as a badge of honor for years. What I didn't realize was that I'd built a whole identity around being the strong one. The safe one. The listener. The fixer. The "I've got you" girl.

But who had me?

It hit hardest in my most intimate relationships. I kept trying to connect, like truly connect. But the version of me I was showing up as, wasn't even real. I was offering a curated version. Watered down. Peacekeeping. Non-threatening.

Because in the past, when I showed too much, too much emotion, too much need, too much truth, even too much laughter, I got shut down. Or worse, punished with distance, told I was too sensitive, told I was too much.

So I adapted. Again.

I became agreeable. Chill. Cool girl energy. The woman who didn't need too much, didn't ask for much, didn't complain. I became the woman who cheered him on while quietly shrinking in the background.

It's easy to confuse proximity with intimacy. But just because someone's close, doesn't mean they *see* you. And if you've trained them to only interact with the version of you that keeps the peace? Then real connection isn't even on the table.

Here's the spiritual punch in the gut: the universe doesn't reward the false self. That version of you that's playing nice just to be loved? She doesn't manifest true alignment. She attracts more situations where she has to keep pretending.

That's why everything started feeling off. Why the conversations felt shallow. Why the sex felt mechanical. Why the friendships felt one-sided. Why I felt so alone, even while being "loved."

Because deep down, I knew I wasn't showing up as *me.* I was performing.

And connection without authenticity is just a performance with an audience that doesn't even know your name.

Real connection, soul connection, only happens when you stop hiding. When you show up fully, even if it's messy. Even if it's "too much." Even if it means someone might walk away.

Because if they walk, they aren't your people anyway.

The illusion of connection is dangerous. It convinces you to stay quiet. It tricks you into thinking this is as good as it gets. It whispers, *"Don't rock the boat."*

But here's the truth: if being fully yourself sinks the boat, then it was never your ship to sail.

Your Turn:

Name one small way you could stop performing and start showing up as your whole damn self today. No big leaps, just one action that feels real.

Imagine the ripple, what doors or connections could open if I showed up with that energy instead of the mask?

CHAPTER FOUR

An Unexpected Messenger

Some people blow into your life for a reason, some for a season, and some for a lifetime. This guy? He was a "reason" person, and his reason was to light the first fuse.

I was in the middle of the emotional hangover that comes after a marriage finally flatlines. We hadn't even signed the papers yet, but it was over. Truth was, it had been over long before the official end. I'd been living as the "perfect wife" for years, agreeable, low-maintenance, easy to manage, which was just code for slowly erasing myself so no one else would have to deal with my edges.

When it was done, I didn't feel free. I didn't feel devastated. I felt... empty. Like someone had taken a Shop-Vac to my soul and left the lights on but stripped the furniture out. One afternoon, I was sitting in a coffee shop, staring into a latte I couldn't taste, when a man I'd never seen before walked up.

Weathered jeans, crow's feet, hands that looked like they'd actually built something. He nodded toward the empty chair.

"Mind if I sit?"

Normally, I'd have given a polite smile and made an excuse. But I didn't have the energy for polite, so I just said, "Sure."

We sat there in silence for a few minutes. Then, without preamble, he said, "You look like someone who's been holding her breath for a very long time."

It wasn't a question. And it went through me like a dart.

I gave a dry laugh. "Yeah, well... oxygen's overrated."

He didn't smile. He just leaned forward slightly. "You know there comes a point where you either keep pretending everything's fine... or you burn the whole damn thing down and start over. Both are hard. Only one will save you."

And there it was, my entire reality, in one sentence from a man I didn't know.

We talked for maybe half an hour. Not about details, not about the divorce, but about the way people disappear inside their own lives. He didn't try to fix me. He didn't pity me. He just dropped truth after truth like it was his job.

When he stood to leave, he said, "Stop waiting for someone to give you permission to live your own damn life."

And then he was gone.

That night, I told my friend Jenelle about the coffee shop encounter. She didn't skip a beat.

"You know who you should talk to?" she said, pulling out her phone. "There's this woman, Dara, some call her a healer, some call her a spiritual alchemist, I just call her the real deal. She helped me when I was in the ugliest chapter of my life. She doesn't coddle you, she doesn't tell you what you want to hear, but she'll help you burn down what needs burning and rebuild something worth living."

I rolled my eyes. "Sounds... intense."

"She is," Jenelle said. "But you're ready for intense."

The next day, I looked her up. No glossy, new-age Instagram aesthetic. No fake guru vibe. Just this grounded, fierce presence in every photo, like she'd walked through fire and didn't feel the need to show off the scars.

Her website was bare bones: a few words about "coming home to yourself," a blurry picture of a forest, and one line that stuck with me:

> *When you're ready to stop abandoning yourself, call me.*

So I did.

We talked for twenty minutes. She didn't ask for the polished backstory; she asked the questions no one else had dared to:

"What's it costing you to keep living like this?"
"When's the last time you told the truth about what you want?"
"Are you ready to stop betraying yourself, or are you still waiting for permission?"

By the end of the call, my hands were shaking. Not because she'd told me what to do, but because she'd reminded me that deep down, I already knew.

When she invited me to a retreat she was hosting in Costa Rica I didn't say yes right away. But the thought of it wouldn't leave me alone. And a week later, I packed my bag.

"I always did something I was a little not ready to do. I think that's how you grow. When there's that moment of 'Wow, I'm not really sure I can do this,' and you push through those moments, that's when you have a breakthrough."

~ *Marissa Mayer*

CHAPTER FIVE

Meeting the Guide

Costa Rica wasn't on my bucket list. It wasn't on *any* list.
I didn't book the ticket because I was chasing some tropical Instagram fantasy. I booked it because the alternative was staying home and sinking deeper into a life I couldn't pretend in anymore. Something deep within me was called to me.

So there I was, stepping off the plane into a wall of heat and air so thick it felt like I could chew it. My hair immediately staged a coup, my clothes stuck to me, and the smell, salt, earth, rain, wrapped itself around me like it knew I was overdue for something real.

The retreat center was tucked in the jungle not far from the beach. No glossy brochures, no infinity pools. Just open-air cabins, hammocks, and the sound of howler monkeys in the distance. I wasn't here for luxury. I was here because Jenelle's mysterious "spiritual alchemist" had told me, "If you come, come ready to work. No hiding, no excuses."

When I finally met her, she wasn't what I expected. No flowy robes, no mystical chanting. Just a woman in worn jeans and a tank top, barefoot in the sand, hair pulled back, eyes like they could strip away every mask you'd ever worn.

"You made it," she said, shaking my hand like we were about to seal a deal.

"Yeah," I replied, trying not to sound defensive. "Figured I'd see what this is about."

She gave me a look like she'd heard that a hundred times and already knew how the story ended. "You'll get out of this exactly what you're willing to put in. Some people come here for a spiritual vacation. They leave with pretty photos. Some come here ready to burn down what's killing them. They leave free."

Her words hit me right in the chest. Not because they were poetic, they weren't, but because they were true.

We sat at a rough wooden table under a thatched roof with the sound of waves in the distance. She didn't ask me to "share my journey" or "speak my truth" she asked questions that cut to the bone:

"What's the biggest lie you're still telling yourself?"
"Who benefits from you staying small?"
"When's the last time you made a decision without checking if it would make everyone else comfortable?"

I wanted to dodge. I wanted to give her the clean, edited answers I'd mastered. But she just waited, steady, eyes locked on mine, like she wasn't going anywhere until I stopped bullshitting.

So I told her. About the marriage. The pretending. The slow bleed of becoming what everyone else needed instead of who I actually am.

When I finished, she didn't give me a pep talk. She just said, "Good. Now we have something to work with. But you're going to have to stop worshiping at the altar of keeping the peace. You can't heal while you're still performing."

That night, lying in the hammock outside my cabin, I kept hearing that one line: *You can't heal while you're still performing.*
And I knew she was right.

I didn't come all the way to the jungle to stay the same.

"Vulnerability is not winning or losing; it's having the courage to show up and be seen when we have no control over the outcome".

~ Brene Brown

CHAPTER SIX

The First Glimpse

The retreat center sat where the jungle met the sea, the kind of place where the air smelled like salt and wet earth. It reminded me of an old girl scout camp in the woods, when I was a child, minus the monkeys and warm ocean.

By the third day, the noise in my head had started to quiet. Not gone, but dulled enough that I could hear things I'd been drowning out for years, the sound of my own breath, the steady thump of my heartbeat, the fact that my shoulders had been up around my ears for about a decade.

That morning, Dara, our guide, led a small group of us down a sandy path to the beach. No ceremony, no long explanation. Just: *"We're walking. Phones stay behind."*

The tide was rolling in, foamy and loud, the water that impossible turquoise you swear is Photoshopped. I kicked off my sandals and stepped into the surf. Warm. Alive. Like it wanted to pull me in.

We walked in silence for a while, and for the first time in... hell, maybe years... I wasn't thinking about who needed me or what was waiting in my inbox. I wasn't adjusting my tone for anyone. I wasn't rehearsing some conversation I'd probably never have. I was just there, sand between my toes, sun on my back, salt on my lips.

At some point, I realized I was smiling. Not the polite, "everything's fine" smile. The real kind, the kind that sneaks up on you before you know it's happening. And it scared the hell out of me because it meant I was still in there somewhere.

Dara must have noticed, because she stopped walking and looked right at me.
"Feels different when you stop dragging your past around, doesn't it?"

I wanted to argue, tell her it wasn't that simple, but she wasn't wrong. Something about that moment felt like a crack in the wall I'd built around myself. Small, but enough for the light to get in.

Later, lying in a hammock strung between two palm trees, I replayed the morning in my head. No big breakthroughs. No fireworks. Just a pause. A breath. And for the first time in a long time, I didn't feel like I was performing.

It felt foreign.

Because after years of disappearing into roles, mom, partner, boss, peacemaker, I didn't even know what it meant to be fully me anymore. I had been a shape-shifter in my own life. Saying yes when I meant no. Staying quiet to avoid conflict. Carrying the emotional weight for everyone while pretending I was fine.

But that day? Something shifted. I sat in stillness long enough to hear my own heartbeat and it hit me like a wave: *I'm still in here.*

Beneath the masks. Beneath the exhaustion. Beneath the layers of *shoulds* and *have-tos* and *what will they think.*

I didn't feel fully alive yet. But I felt aware. That I was here. That I mattered. That I wasn't just a background character in my own story.

And here's the truth that caught me off guard: I didn't need to become someone new. I needed to return to who I was before the world told me who to be.

Before I dimmed my light in relationships just to keep the peace.
Before I disconnected from my own body to survive the pressure.

Before I traded my voice for approval, my boundaries for belonging.

There had been a time when I moved through the world with certainty, not arrogance, but a grounded kind of knowing. I didn't question my value. I didn't need outside validation. I trusted what I felt.

Somewhere along the way, I lost that. Bit by bit. Year by year. Compromise by compromise.

But it wasn't gone. Just buried.

And that glimpse? It reminded me: I wasn't broken. I wasn't lost. I had just forgotten.

Forgotten that I'm not just a body moving through the world, I'm something deeper. A soul with grit. A spirit that knows. A light that never went out, even if it got covered in dust.

People call it different things, intuition, inner voice, divine spark. I don't care what label you put on it. I just know this: we all have it. And when we lose touch with it, we feel numb, disconnected, hollow. Like we're walking through life in grayscale. For the first time, I wondered if all those years of numbness weren't random at all, but symptoms of Disconnected Self

Syndrome, proof that I had been drifting away from myself long before I noticed

That morning, standing in the surf, I saw myself in color for the first time in a long while.

And I knew right then: I wasn't going back.

Your Turn:

When's the last time you felt fully alive in your body, not hustling, not pleasing, just being? Write about it. Then write one thing you can do this week to feel that way again.

Infusion: Anchor it in the now: if I held that feeling in my body daily, what experiences would naturally be drawn to me?

____

____

____

____

____

____

____

____

____

____

____

CHAPTER SEVEN

The Old Skin

By the fourth day, the place had gotten under my skin, in every way.

I'd stopped checking the time. My makeup bag stayed zipped. I could tell the hour by the way the sun hit the water and the smell of whatever the kitchen was cooking. Mornings were heavy with coffee and damp air; afternoons tasted like salt and mango. Nights were warm, dark, and loud with insects that didn't care if you slept.

Dara said today was about *"dropping the old skin."*

I hated how that sounded, like some woo-woo snake ritual. but I knew exactly what she meant.

There comes a moment when you realize the version of you that's been walking through the world... isn't really you. It's the version you built to stay safe. The one who knew how to read a room before she ever accesses her own needs. The one who made herself smaller, quieter, more agreeable, because too much of her always seemed to be a problem.

She was necessary. She got me through some hard chapters. She learned how to smile through discomfort, to show up even when she wanted to disappear. She wore strength like armor and silence like a badge of honor. But she wasn't me. Not really.

She was the collection of every expectation I absorbed. Every time I was told to calm down, be nice, lower my voice, make it work, be grateful it's not worse. Every time I ignored my gut to keep the peace. Every time I swallowed my truth to protect someone else's comfort. Every time I betrayed myself just to be chosen.

I knew what Dara meant because that version of me knew how to survive, but not how to live fully in my own skin.

We met on the beach just after sunrise. The tide was low, leaving behind wide stretches of smooth sand. Dara told us to find a spot alone and write down every role, mask, or identity we were done carrying.

At first, I sat there with the pen hovering, trying to make it neat. Then something in me snapped, and the list started pouring out:
The "cool wife." The "strong one." The "good boss." The "understanding friend." The "woman who never needs help." The "everything's fine" actress.

By the time I stopped, the paper was full. My hand ached. My throat felt tight.

"Now," Dara said, *"read it out loud. To the ocean."*

Now I have to tell you, that felt a bit strange. What the hell was that going to do? I did it anyway because something inside said to trust her.

I stood there, bare feet in the surf, the sun just high enough to warm my shoulders. My voice cracked on the first few lines, but I kept going. With each one, I felt lighter, and also like I might throw up. Saying it out loud made it real.

When I finished, Dara handed me a lighter.
"Your old skin doesn't get to come home with you."

The air was still, the flame steady. The paper curled and blackened in my hand, and I dropped it into the waves. The ashes swirled, broke apart, and disappeared.

And just like that, nothing magical happened. No lightning bolt, no choir of angels. Just me, standing there with wet feet and an empty hand.

But here's the thing about shedding the old skin: it isn't glamorous. It's gritty. Disorienting. Terrifying.

Even though it doesn't fit anymore, it's familiar, and familiar feels safe, even when it's suffocating. Your nervous system gets used to feeling a certain way, and stepping out of it feels uncomfortable, even unsafe.

When I started shedding, it wasn't with some big declaration. It was in the quiet choices. Saying no when I usually said yes. Walking away instead of twisting myself into another emotional pretzel. Letting myself not be liked. Letting myself not explain.

And every time I did, something loosened.

That old skin clung to me like a second layer of shame. But the more I moved toward the part of me I'd disconnected from, the more it cracked.

This process? It isn't about becoming someone new. It's about un-becoming everything you were never meant to be. It's remembering that strength doesn't always look like endurance. Sometimes it looks like honesty. Rest. Boundaries. Saying, *this isn't working for me anymore*, even if your voice shakes. Trusting yourself even when no one else understands your choices.

Later, walking back up the beach, I realized I was standing taller. Breathing deeper. The space where that list used to live inside me felt… open.

And for the first time, I wanted to see what could fill it.

Because the old skin wasn't my identity.
It was my armor.
And I was finally ready to take it off.

"We cultivate love when we allow our most vulnerable and powerful selves to be deeply seen and known, and when we honor the spiritual connection that grows from that offering with trust, respect, kindness and affection.

Love is not something we give or get; it is something that we nurture and grow, a connection that can only be cultivated between two people when it exists within each one of them – we can only love others as much as we love ourselves.

Shame, blame, disrespect, betrayal, and the withholding of affection damage the roots from which love grows. Love can only survive these injuries if they are acknowledged, healed and rare."

~ Brené Brown, The Gifts of Imperfection

CHAPTER EIGHT

Rise of the Real Me

It didn't happen all at once. There wasn't a flash of lightning or some magical moment when everything clicked into place.

It was more like a quiet rebellion.
A subtle, steady refusal to keep living a life that didn't feel like mine anymore.

By the fifth day, my body was buzzing with it, the truth I'd swallowed for years. The tight jaw. The locked shoulders. The stomach that clenched every time I bit my tongue instead of speaking up. Dara called it *truth weight*, the heaviness that lives in your body when you choose silence over honesty.

That afternoon, she pulled me aside after a group session. *"Let's walk,"* she said.

We headed down the narrow path toward the water, the air thick with the smell of rain and salt. At the edge of the beach, she stopped and faced me.
"What haven't you said?"

I laughed it off. *"Where do you want me to start?"*

"Where it hurts most," she said, dead serious.

My chest tightened like a vice. I wanted to run. But there was no point in coming all this way if I wasn't going to be real.

So I told her. About the resentment I'd swallowed. About all the times I'd made someone else's comfort matter more than my truth. About the nights I'd lay awake, replaying conversations I never had the courage to start. About how I'd learned to shrink my needs small enough to fit inside someone else's life.

By the time I stopped, my voice was hoarse. My eyes burned, but I wasn't crying. Not yet.

Dara didn't blink. *"You think silence kept you safe. But it didn't. It kept you invisible."*

That hit me like a wave. I'd been so focused on surviving, the marriage, the business, the image, that I hadn't noticed how completely I'd disappeared.

"Say one thing out loud right now that you've been afraid to admit," she pressed.

I stared at the horizon, the sun slipping lower, the water catching fire in its glow. My throat felt like it might close. And then I said it, a truth so raw I couldn't believe it came out of my mouth.

The moment the words hit the air, my whole body let go. Tears ripped through me. My knees buckled until I was sitting in the wet sand, waves lapping at my legs. Dara didn't comfort me. She didn't need to. She just stood there as a witness, letting the ocean take what I'd been carrying.

When it passed, I wasn't fixed. I wasn't healed. But I was lighter. Like I'd finally set down a bag I wasn't meant to carry in the first place.

And something shifted.

Because here's the thing: the first time you tell the real truth out loud, not the sugarcoated version, not the softened version for everyone else's comfort, it's not polished, it's not pretty. But damn, it's powerful.

For so long, I'd measured my worth by how well I held everything together. How selfless I could be. But beneath the performance, I was exhausted. Hollow. I used to think selflessness was noble. Now I see it for what it was: fear.

Fear that if I stopped being the caretaker, the fixer, the one who never needed anything, no one would stay.

Fear that my enough-ness was tied to what I could do for others, not who I was.

So I started testing the waters. I said no. I admitted when I was tired, hurt, or didn't have the answer. And guess what? The world didn't end. The ones who truly loved me leaned in closer. Others? They disappeared.

It stung, but it also set me free.

Because I realized I didn't want to be loved for the version of me that made other people's lives easier. I wanted to be loved for the woman who was real, messy, magical, still figuring it out.

Each time I told the truth, each time I followed that inner nudge instead of gaslighting myself, the real me stepped forward. She wasn't polished. She wasn't perfect. But she was strong as hell. A little wild. Grounded. Done apologizing for existing.

There's something sacred about rising, not as the version you think you should be, but as the raw, heart-led woman you actually are. The one who's not afraid to disrupt the status quo. The one who's done begging life to feel better and is finally making it better, not by force, but by alignment.

And yes, it's lonely sometimes. Not everyone claps for you when you stop playing their game. But for the first time in a long time, I can look in the mirror and recognize the woman staring back.

She's not perfect. She doesn't have it all figured out. But she's here. Fully. Unapologetically. Powerfully present.

And that's more than enough.

Your Turn:

What's the one truth you've been biting your tongue about? Write it down, uncensored, no sugarcoating. Then ask: who would I be if I stopped letting fear keep me quiet?

Infusion: And if I embodied that fearless version of me, what reality would I begin to attract, and how soon could I start living it?

___

___

___

___

___

___

___

___

___

___

___

CHAPTER NINE

Letting Go of the Armor

By the last full day in Costa Rica, I'd started to notice something strange: I could breathe.

Not the shallow, on-edge kind of breathing I'd gotten used to, real, steady breaths that reached all the way down. The kind that made my shoulders drop and my jaw unclench without me even thinking about it.

It's wild how you don't realize the armor you've been wearing until you start taking it off. Mine wasn't made of steel, it was made of sarcasm, deflection, keeping busy, and never letting anyone see how much I actually cared. It had served me well in boardrooms and bad relationships, but it was heavy as hell.

That morning, Dara told us to meet at the beach before sunrise. She loved having us wake up with the sun. Thankfully it was something I was used to. The tide was out, leaving wide pools of still water that mirrored the pink and gold sky. She handed each of us a smooth stone.

"This," she said, "is the thing you still haven't let go of. You know what it is. You've been carrying it a long time. Name it. Then give it back to the ocean."

I turned the stone in my palm. I knew exactly what mine was. It wasn't the divorce. It wasn't the business stress. It was the belief that I had to handle everything alone, that if I needed help, I was weak, and if I showed pain, I'd lose respect. It was the Vow my soul made as a child when I realized it wasn't safe to be me on this planet. I remember the moments well. I was being my joyful playful self and my dad yelled at me to be quiet. He said that a lot! I vowed at that moment that I would make everyone happy and do everything myself.

Dara stood in front of me. "Say it," she said.

"I don't have to carry it all," I said quietly. Then louder: "I don't have to carry it all."

The words didn't feel small. They felt like they cracked something open in me.

I walked into the surf until the water reached my knees. The waves were warm, steady, and alive. I opened my hand and let the stone drop. I watched it vanish.

The minute it left my palm, I felt it, the space. Not like I was suddenly lighter and free forever, but like I'd made a conscious choice to stop dragging a piece of my own prison around.

As I walked back to shore, the sun broke fully over the horizon, lighting up the water like it was on fire. I didn't feel broken. I didn't feel fragile. I felt strong, not because I was armored up, but because I wasn't.

That's when I realized: strength isn't about holding it together at all costs. Real strength is letting yourself be seen without the walls.

Your Turn:

What piece of armor have you been wearing so long you've forgotten what it's protecting? What would it take to set it down?

Infusion: Then visualize: with that weight gone, what new opportunities, relationships, or joy could flow into my field?

___

___

___

___

___

___

___

___

___

___

___

CHAPTER TEN

Meeting Her Future Self

On the last night of the retreat, Dara asked us to meet by the water just before sunset, again. What was she going to have us do now? Was there more? The tide was high, the waves rolling in steady, the air thick with that electric smell that comes right before a storm.

We sat in a loose circle on the sand. Dara passed around small candles in glass jars. "We're going to meet someone tonight," she said. "Not me. Not each other. You're going to meet the version of yourself who's already living the life you say you want."

The old me would have rolled my eyes at that. But after a week here, I knew better, and it felt right.

She had us close our eyes and breathe, slow and deep, matching the rhythm of the waves. Then she said, "See her. Not the fantasy, not the Instagram-perfect version, the real one. The one who's been through it, who knows who she is, and who stopped apologizing for it a long time ago."

I saw her immediately.
Bare feet on the deck of a small house by the ocean. Sun in her hair. Laugh lines deeper, stronger. A body that looked like it'd been used, for dancing, for hugging, for living, not just for show. She was

grounded. Certain. Her eyes... God, her eyes. They weren't tired anymore.

She moved through her day with ease, not because her life was perfect, but because she trusted herself. She didn't chase approval. She didn't play small. She didn't waste energy proving her worth, she just *lived it.*

And then she looked right at me. And I swear I could hear her say, *Stop waiting to become me. Start now.*

When Dara told us to open our eyes, the sky was on fire, orange, pink, deep purple. The storm had passed us by. My candle was still burning.

I didn't feel like I'd met a stranger. I felt like I'd remembered someone I used to know. And this time, I wasn't letting her go.

As I walked back to my cabin, I knew I'd be heading home the next day with more than just stories. I was leaving with a map, not of steps and checklists, but of how it feels to live as her.

And once you've felt that, you can't un-feel it.

Your Turn:

Picture the you, who's already living the life you want. What's one thing she does differently than you do now, and how can you start doing it today?

CHAPTER ELEVEN

Returning Home

The first thing I noticed when I walked into my house was how damn quiet it was.
Not the good kind of quiet, not ocean waves or jungle birds.
This was dead quiet. Heavy. The kind that makes you instantly aware you're back in the land of bills, deadlines, and people who expect you to answer their texts before they finish typing them.

Everything was exactly where I'd left it. The perfect furniture arrangement. The matching pillows. The countertops, so clean you could eat off them. And suddenly it all felt staged, like the set of a show I didn't even want to star in anymore.

Then the phone started lighting up.

Can you jump on a call?
We need your notes on the project.
Hey, can you watch the kids this weekend?

By the third one, my gut reaction was automatic: say yes, fix it, handle it, prove I'm still reliable. That old muscle memory is strong.

I reached for the phone... then stopped. My Costa Rica self, barefoot, salty hair, breathing easy, would not be jumping back into this circus before she even unpacked.

So I set the phone down. And yeah, it was harder than it should've been. My hands itched to pick it back up. My brain kept whispering, *What if they think you're unreliable now?*

I made tea instead. Sat by the window. I tried to pretend I didn't hear the little voice saying, *You know this silence won't last.*

Because it didn't.

Within hours, it started: the passive-aggressive "Hope everything's okay" emails. The guilt-trips disguised as "checking in." The expectation that my return meant I was back to being on-demand.

For a minute, I wavered. I almost caved. I almost slid right back into the role I'd played so damn well, the one where I show up for everyone else before I even figure out what I need.

But I didn't get on a plane, sweat my ass off in the jungle, and pour my guts out to the ocean just to come home and shrink again.

So I called one person back. One. And I told them exactly what I could do and what I couldn't. No apologies. No softening the edges to make it palatable.

There was a pause. I could practically hear them recalculating their opinion of me. But they said "Okay." And the world didn't end.

It wasn't a massive win. It wasn't a Hollywood transformation. But it was one choice in the right direction. And that's how this works, one choice at a time.

"Awareness doesn't mean the pattern never shows up. It means you know it when it does and chose something else"

CHAPTER TWELVE

The First Test

It didn't take long for the universe to throw me a curveball.
Forty-eight hours after I got home, I walked into the office thinking I'd ease back in. Check emails. Catch up. Maybe grab lunch with my assistant and tell her about monkeys stealing bananas at breakfast.

Instead, I walked straight into a storm.

Amy, my marketing director, was waiting in my office looking like she'd been chewing on a lemon for three days. "We've got a problem," she said. Then she unloaded it: a client was furious, the team was scrambling, and somehow, according to the narrative being passed around, it was *my* mess to clean up.

The old me would've jumped right in, smoothed every ruffled feather, fixed it all before anyone could think I'd dropped the ball. That knee-jerk urge was still there, buzzing in my chest.

But Costa Rica, me? She was standing in the back of my mind with her arms crossed, saying, *You don't have to carry it all.*

I took a breath. Sat down. "Okay," I said slowly. "Walk me through what's already been done to solve this."

Amy, blinked at me. She was expecting me to start spinning plates, not hand the wheel back.

As she talked, I could feel the old reflex fighting to break through, the one that said, *Do it yourself, do it faster, do it perfectly so no one can blame you.* My hands were practically twitching. When she finished, I nodded. "Sounds like you've got a plan. Let me know if you hit a wall you can't get past. Otherwise, I trust you to handle it." Her eyes widened like I just told her I was joining the circus. "You... don't want to take it over?" "No," I said. "I want you to handle it. You're capable. That's why you're here."

She left my office looking a little stunned but also... taller somehow. And for the rest of the day, I watched her own it. Not just ticking boxes, but making decisions, taking initiative, rallying the team. I saw her step into the role I'd been holding her back from without even realizing it.

That's when it hit me: I'd created a culture where my team leaned on me for everything because I'd trained them to. I'd made myself the safety net, the fixer, the one with all the answers, which kept them dependent and kept me drowning.

Letting go didn't just free up my mental space; it gave her a chance to lead. And watching her rise to it? That felt better than any perfectly executed rescue mission I'd ever pulled off.

Driving home, I realized this was leadership. Not hoarding control, not micromanaging to prove my worth, but trusting people enough to let them shine. Delegating wasn't just going to make my life 100% better, it was going to make *them* better too.

And that's the thing: real leaders don't just run the show. They build more leaders.

"The sooner we let go of holding on, the sooner we can hold on to the beauty of what's unfolding before us."

~ Julieanne O'Connor

CHAPTER THIRTEEN

Bloodline Boundaries

It's one thing to hold your ground at work. It's another thing entirely when it's family because they've known you your whole life and they know *exactly* which buttons to push.

I hadn't even been home from Costa Rica a week when my phone lit up with my sister's name.
"Hey," she said without so much as a hello. "I need you to come over Saturday. Mom's freaking out about the fundraiser. We have to do all the centerpieces, and you're the only one who can make it look right."

Old me? Would've said yes before she even finished. I would've rearranged my whole weekend, canceled whatever I had going on, and shown up with my sleeves rolled, doing the work while quietly resenting every second.

Instead, I paused. Not because I didn't want to help, I love my mom, but because I knew this pattern. My sister doesn't *ask*, she *assigns*, and I've always played along.

"I can't this Saturday," I said, keeping my voice calm. "I already have plans, I'm not moving."

Silence. The kind that drips with judgment. Then: "Seriously? This is for Mom. She's stressed out of her mind. We always do this together."

I could feel the guilt creeping in, whispering all the usual lines: *Don't be selfish. It's family. Just do it.* But that woman I met in Costa Rica, the one who stopped living for everyone else's approval, was in my head saying, *Don't fold. Set the terms.*

So I added, "But I can help on Thursday evening if that works. I can come over after work, bring what we need, and knock out a good chunk so Saturday isn't so overwhelming for you guys."

Another pause. This one wasn't as sharp. I could almost hear her recalculating.
"Okay," she said finally. "Yeah, Thursday could work."

"Great," I said. And I meant it. Because now I was helping in a way that actually worked for me, not dropping everything just because someone expected me to.

When I hung up, I realized something big: boundaries don't have to mean slamming the door shut. They can mean opening it *on your terms*. And with family, that might just be the difference between resentment and real connection.

(When I hung up, my hands were shaking. Part of me felt like the worst daughter and sister on the planet. But another part, the stronger part, felt something I hadn't felt in years: pride.

Because here's the truth no one wants to say out loud, if you never set boundaries with your family, they will keep you in the same role you've played since you were a kid. And you'll keep living a life built for their comfort instead of your own.

I wasn't willing to do that anymore).

"Daring to set boundaries is about having the courage to love ourselves, even when we risk disappointing others."

"If someone throws a fit because you set boundaries, it's just more evidence the boundary is needed."

~Brene Brown

CHAPTER FOURTEEN

The Crash

Change is exhausting. No one talks about that part.

You think you'll come home from a life-altering retreat and just float through life on a cloud of zen. The truth? You're breaking habits that have had a death grip on you for years, and every single choice feels like lifting weights you've never trained for.

Two weeks after Costa Rica, I crashed.

It started small, a couple of late nights at work, skipping my morning walk, letting my phone creep back into my hand before I'd even gotten out of bed. Then the mental noise started up again: *You're not doing enough. You're letting people down. This isn't going to last.*

One night, I sat at my kitchen counter staring at my laptop, three cups of cold coffee in front of me, a to-do list that looked like it had been breeding, and that old tightness in my chest making a comeback.

I'd been so proud of holding my boundaries, at work, with my sister, even with myself. But now I felt like I was right back in the spin cycle.

For a split second, I thought about calling the spiritual alchemist from the retreat, half to get advice, half to confess that maybe I wasn't cut out for this "new me" thing after all.

Instead, I shut the laptop, poured the coffee down the sink, and sat in the dark. I let myself feel it: the exhaustion, the frustration, the temptation to throw it all out the window and just go back to being who everyone expected me to be.

And here's the ugly truth: part of me wanted to. Because at least that version of me didn't have to fight for every damn choice.

But the other part, the part that stood barefoot on that deck in Costa Rica, reminded me of something Dara said on the last day of the retreat:

"Your old life will always be right there, waiting for you. The question is, are you willing to do what it takes to keep walking toward the one you actually want?"

That hit hard.

I went to bed early that night. No victory lap, no perfect morning routine the next day. Just rest. And when I woke up, I made one small, solid choice in the right direction. Because maybe that's all this really is, one choice at a time, even on the days you feel like you're failing.

"Your assumption, to be effective, cannot be a single isolated act; it must be a maintained attitude."

- Neville Goddard

CHAPTER FIFTEEN

The Spark

It was a Tuesday afternoon, the kind where nothing in particular is wrong but everything feels… flat.

I was sitting at my desk, half-watching the clock, half-scrolling through emails I didn't care about, when a notification popped up.

Subject: Hey, you.

It was from Marisol, the woman I'd met the second night of the retreat in Costa Rica. The one who made me laugh so hard during the group circle that I nearly spit my tea across the deck.
We hadn't talked since the plane ride home.

I was just thinking about you today, the email said. *Remember that sunrise swim? The one where you swore you couldn't get in because it was too cold, and then you dove in headfirst? I think about that a lot. You're braver than you give yourself credit for.*

I sat back in my chair, reading it twice. Three times.

It wasn't a big speech. It wasn't even meant to be life changing. But it hit me hard because I'd been forgetting. Forgetting the courage, it took to sign up for that retreat in the first place. Forgetting the woman who stood on the shore that morning, shivering but smiling, knowing the only way forward was in.

Marisol added one last line:
I'm planning a beach weekend next month. No pressure, but if you're up for some saltwater therapy, I'd love to see you there.

I didn't reply right away. I just sat there, feeling that spark in my chest, the one that had been dimming under the weight of my to-do list.

By the end of the day, I'd written her back: *Count me in.*

It wasn't about the beach. It was about saying yes to something that reminded me who I was becoming. And maybe that's the real secret, when the world starts pulling you back into who you used to be, you have to keep putting yourself in places, and around people, that make it impossible to forget who you're meant to be.

You become the five people you surround yourself with. If you want to change you have to change the people you surround yourself with.

Your Turn:

Who's someone in your life who sees the best version of you, and reminds you of it when you've forgotten? When's the last time you reached out to them?

CHAPTER SIXTEEN

Proof of Life

The second my feet hit the sand, I felt it, that deep exhale I didn't even know I'd been holding.

The ocean in front of me was a solid sheet of silver under the late afternoon sun, and the sound of waves made my whole nervous system unclench. Marisol was already there, sprawled out on a blanket with two cold drinks and a grin.

"Thought you'd bail," she teased.

"Almost did," I admitted, dropping my bag. "Then I realized I didn't want to listen to my own excuses anymore."

We fell into easy conversation, the kind where you don't have to fill every silence because the ocean's doing the talking. That night we built a driftwood fire, laughed until our faces hurt, and let the tide decide when we should call it.

The next morning, Marisol shook me awake before sunrise. "C'mon, let's swim," she said, shoving a towel in my face.

The water was colder than I remembered. The kind of cold that makes your whole body argue with you. Old me would've dipped a toe in, shivered dramatically, and then volunteered to be "the towel holder."

But I didn't even hesitate. I dove.

The shock hit me like a punch, then dissolved into adrenaline and laughter. Salt water in my mouth, hair plastered to my face, waves tossing me around like they owned me, and all I could think was *I'm here. I'm in it.*

When I finally crawled back to shore, lungs burning, I saw Marisol watching me with that same grin she'd had in Costa Rica. "See? Still the woman who dives in headfirst."

That's when it clicked. I wasn't here proving anything to her. I was proving it to myself, that I wasn't just talking about change anymore. I was living it, in all the small, stubborn ways that add up.

I wrapped up in my towel, stared at the horizon, and thought, *This is the life I came here for.* Not perfect. Not constant sunshine. But mine.

"Always concentrate on how far you have come, rather than how far you have left to go. The difference in how easy it seems will amaze you."

~ Heidi Johnson

CHAPTER SEVENTEEN

The Leap

The Monday after the beach weekend, I walked into the office with sand still stuck in the bottom of my bag and a new kind of calm in my chest.

That lasted until lunch.

Amy knocked on my door, closed it behind her, and sat down like she was bracing for impact.
"So... there's an opportunity I think you should know about," she said carefully.

Turns out a major client wanted to expand their contract, *if* we could take on a project twice the size of anything we'd done before. Which meant more visibility, more revenue, and more risk.

Old me would've gone one of two ways:

1. Agree immediately out of fear of missing out, then kill myself making it perfect.

2. Politely decline because "now's not a good time," and watch someone else take the shot.

But I just sat there, listening. I could feel that familiar cocktail of excitement and terror swirling in my gut, and underneath it, something new. A steadiness.

"What's your gut say?" Amy asked.

"My gut says we can do it," I said. "But not the old way."

I laid it out: We'd take it, but we'd restructure the workflow, so it didn't burn us out. Everyone would have clear roles, no heroics, no martyrdom. I'd stay in my lane as the leader, not the cleanup crew.

Amy grinned. "So... we're saying yes?"

"Hell yes," I said.

When she left, I leaned back in my chair and realized what had just happened. I'd made a bold choice without the panic, without the overpromising, without selling my soul for approval.

That's the thing about braver, it's not just cliff jumps or ocean dives. Sometimes it's sitting in a meeting, looking at a big, scary opportunity, and deciding you're damn well ready for it... on your terms.

Your Turn:

What's the big thing you've been circling, waiting for the 'right time'? Write what it would look like to say yes to it now, but on your terms, without burning yourself out.

Ask yourself: if I said yes now, how would the Universe rearrange to meet me? What's the first aligned step I can take to call that reality closer?

CHAPTER EIGHTEEN

The Conversation That Changed Everything

It had been weeks since I left Costa Rica, but the sound of the waves and the smell of saltwater still lived somewhere in my bones.

I'd thought about calling Dara, a dozen times since I got back, usually in the middle of the night when my brain wouldn't shut up. I kept telling myself I didn't *need* to. That I was fine. That I was "handling it."

But that Monday night, after the meeting about the big new client, I finally picked up the phone.

She answered on the second ring, her voice warm but no-nonsense. "I was wondering when you'd call."

I laughed. "What, you've got some psychic hotline over there?"

"Not psychic," she said. "Just know the rhythm of growth. You've been in action mode. Now you're ready to integrate."

I told her everything, the boundaries at work, the showdown with my sister, the crash, the spark from Marisol, the ocean swim, the leap at work. She listened without interrupting, but I could tell she was tracking every detail.

When I finally stopped, she asked one question that knocked the air out of me:
"So when are you going to stop treating this as an experiment and start treating it as your life?"

I didn't have an answer.

Because she was right. Somewhere in my head, I'd still been thinking of this as a "phase." A test run. Like at any moment, the old me could slip back in and take over.

"You've been making brave choices," she said. "But bravery isn't about moments. It's about identity. Who you *are*. The woman who draws her own lines. The woman who dives in. The woman who says yes to the right things and no to the rest, without guilt."

I could feel it sinking in. Not like lightning, but like an anchor finding the ocean floor.

"Own it," she said. "Stop looking for proof you've changed. Live like it's already done."

When I hung up, I didn't feel fireworks or some dramatic shift. I felt... grounded. Steady. Like I'd been walking on a shaky bridge and finally set foot on solid ground.

And for the first time, I stopped wondering if I could keep this up.
I knew I could.

"When you remain consistent your vibration stabilizes, your identity solidifies and physical reality begins to bend."

~ Abdullah

CHAPTER NINETEEN

The Test

It's easy to be the "new you" when things are rolling along. The real test comes when life grabs you by the collar and says, *Let's see if you really meant it.*

Mine came on a Thursday.

I was walking out of a meeting, feeling good about a pitch that had gone better than expected, when my phone buzzed. It was my mom.

"Your dads in the ER," she said before I even said hello. "They think it's his heart."

Everything in me wanted to drop my bag, cancel the rest of my day, and sprint into crisis mode. That's how I've always handled family emergencies, full takeover. Call the doctors. Manage the insurance. Stay at the hospital until I'm half-dead myself.

But somewhere between the pounding in my ears and the elevator doors closing, I remembered what Dara had said: *Stop treating this like an experiment. This is your life.*

That meant taking care of my dad *and* myself.

"I'm on my way," I told my mom. "But here's the plan: I'll come for a few hours tonight, then I'm going home to sleep. Tomorrow morning, I'll be back. In the meantime, I'll make sure the boys know what's going on so they can rotate with us."

It felt unnatural. Wrong, even. Like I was shirking my role as the family rock.

When I walked into the hospital, Dad was sitting up, irritated at the fuss, already arguing with the nurse about the heart monitor. Relief hit me so hard my knees almost buckled.

We talked. We laughed. I listened to him complain about the Jell-O. And when the clock hit the time, I'd promised myself I'd leave, I stood up.

"You don't have to stay?" he asked.

"Nope," I said. "You're in good hands. I'll be back in the morning."

Driving home, the old guilt tried to claw its way in. But under it was something stronger: respect for myself.

Because here's the truth, if I'd stayed all night, no one would've told me to go home. They would've praised me. But I would've been exhausted, resentful, and back in the cycle I swore I was done with.

That night, I slept. The next morning, I showed up fresh, clear-headed, and ready to actually help. And my dad? He said it was the most relaxed he'd seen me in years.

Turns out, boundaries don't just protect *you,* they make you better for the people you love.

"You can be a good person with a kind heart and still say no to people."

~ Tracy A. Malone

CHAPTER TWENTY

The Decision

Big decisions don't always announce themselves. Sometimes they slip in quietly, like a stray thought you can't shake.

For me, it started on a Tuesday morning. I was sipping coffee, staring out the window, when the question landed:

What if I just... did it?

"It" had been sitting on the back burner for years, the dream of starting my own consultancy. Not just running someone else's vision, but building my own. Every time it crept into my mind before, I'd shove it away with a long list of reasons why it wasn't the right time. Too much risk. Too many bills. Too many people depending on me.

But now, the excuses sounded thin. Weak, even.

I'd been proving to myself for months that I could lead without burning out, make brave choices without imploding, and live by my own rules. So why was I still playing small?

I grabbed a notebook and started writing. Not a fluffy vision board list. Cold, hard details:

- What I'd offer.
- Who I'd work with.
- How much money I'd need to cover my expenses for six months.
- Which clients I could realistically take with me.

By the time I looked up, the page was full, and it didn't look like a fantasy. It looked like a plan.

That night, I called my coach, Dara. "I think I'm ready," I said.

"Ready for what?" she asked, even though I'm pretty sure she already knew.

"To bet on myself."

There was a pause, then: "Then the only question is, when?"

We talked logistics, timelines, and contingencies. But under all of it, there was this steady hum in my chest, the knowing that I wasn't going to talk myself out of this one.

Two weeks later, I handed in my notice. Not in a blaze of glory, not out of anger, but with the calm certainty of someone who knows exactly what they're walking toward.

Because here's the thing: every "no" I'd said, every boundary I'd held, every brave dive into the unknown had been leading me here.

And now? There was no going back.

Your Turn:

How would it feel in your body if you made the decision to do what has always been in your heart to do?

CHAPTER TWENTY-ONE

New Territory

The first Monday of my new life felt strange. No commute. No staff meetings. No office politics. Just me, my laptop, and the sound of the neighbor's lawnmower.

I'd imagined it would feel like freedom, and it did, but it also felt like standing on a high dive, toes curled over the edge, wondering if the water was as deep as you thought.

The first week was a blur of client calls, emails, and setting up systems. There were moments I caught myself thinking, *What the hell have you done?* But every time that voice piped up, I reminded myself: *This is who you are now. The woman who bets on herself.*

By Friday, I was running on equal parts adrenaline and coffee when Marisol texted:

Beach day tomorrow. Sunrise swim. Bring that headfirst energy.

Part of me wanted to say no, I had a dozen things I "should" be doing. But I'd promised myself this new life wouldn't just be about work.

So I went.

The morning was cool, the sand damp from the tide. I spotted Marisol down the beach, waving me over, and next to her was a guy I didn't know. Tall. Easy smile. The kind of presence that didn't crowd you, just... fit.

"This is Alex," she said. "He's a photographer. I thought you two should meet."

We talked as the sun came up, about travel, work, the weird mix of freedom and fear that comes with starting over. He listened the way people do when they're actually interested, not just waiting for their turn to talk.

When it was time to swim, he grinned. "First one in, has bragging rights."

It wasn't a line. It was a challenge. And I couldn't resist. I dove, salt stinging my skin, hair whipping around my face. When I surfaced, he was right there beside me, laughing.

It wasn't a lightning bolt. No violins. Just a flicker, a reminder that maybe my heart, like the rest of me, was ready for something new.

Later, as we wrapped in towels and sipped coffee on the sand, he asked for my number. I didn't overthink it. I didn't run the mental background check I used to. I just said yes.

Driving home, I realized this was exactly why I'd built this new life, so I'd have space for moments like this. Space to work on my own terms. Space to breathe. And maybe... space to let someone in again.

Your Turn:

What would it feel like to open your heart fully while standing in your newfound confidence and the joy of being you?

CHAPTER TWENTY-TWO

Holding It All

Three weeks into running my own business, I realized something: freedom doesn't mean "easy." It means *choice.*
And choice comes with responsibility.

Some days I nailed it, landing a new client, sending invoices, feeling like the CEO of my own damn life. Other days I found myself staring at the ceiling at 2 a.m., wondering if I'd made the biggest mistake of my career.

The difference now? I didn't spiral. I took a breath, looked at the facts, and kept moving.

In the middle of all that, there was Alex. We'd met for coffee twice since the beach. No pressure. No assumptions. Just two people seeing what might be there. The old me would've been halfway to planning our future by now, or halfway to sabotaging it.

Instead, I let it be light. I told him when I was available, not squeezing him into the cracks of an overstuffed life. And here's the kicker, he respected it. No games. No guilt trips. Just, "Cool, I'll see you then."

One night after dinner, he walked me to my car and said, "You've got this energy like you're in the middle of building something big."

I laughed. "I am. My life."

And I meant it.

That's when I saw it, how the work with Dara, the boundaries, the ocean dives, the leaps at work, the decision to start my own business... it wasn't a collection of separate wins. It was one big shift.

I was no longer living on autopilot. I was *choosing*.

Choosing which clients to take.
Choosing who to spend time with.
Choosing what kind of partner I wanted, and what kind of partner I would be.

The more I chose, the more the noise in my head quieted. Not because everything was perfect, far from it, but because I trusted myself to handle whatever came next.

As I drove home that night, windows down, music up, I realized this was the life I'd been trying to build for years without knowing it. Not one I escaped into on vacation, but one I lived every damn day.

And that, more than anything, felt like freedom.

"As you change your concept of yourself, your world changes accordingly."

~ Joseph Murphy

CHAPTER TWENTY-THREE

Now It's Your Turn

If you'd told me a year ago that I'd be here, running my own business, waking up without dread, feeling genuinely excited about the next chapter, I would've smiled politely and thought, *Yeah, sure.*

Because back then, I was the queen of holding it all together for everyone else while quietly crumbling inside. My boundaries were suggestions. My worth was measured by how much I could do for others. My heart was locked in a vault, "for my own protection."

And then, piece by piece, I started chipping away at that old version of me.

The retreat in Costa Rica cracked me open. The Coach I almost didn't call reminded me who the hell I was. The boundaries, awkward, messy, and sometimes scary, gave me back my time, my sanity, and my dignity.

I learned that bravery isn't about one big leap. It's the dozens of small choices you make every day to live in alignment with who you want to be.
It's telling your family you'll be there, but on a day that works for you.
It's walking into a hospital, loving your dad fiercely, and still going home to sleep.

It's saying yes to a big opportunity without saying no to yourself.
It's handing in your notice because you finally believe you can build something better.

And somewhere along the way, I stopped trying to "prove" I'd changed. I just... lived it.

Now, my days aren't perfect. My business has hiccups. Relationships still require courage. Life still throws curveballs. But the difference is, I trust myself to navigate them. I know when to dive in, when to delegate, and when to walk away.

The other night, Alex asked me, "Do you ever wish you'd done all this sooner?"

I thought about it. Sure, there's a part of me that wishes I'd had these tools years ago. But then I realized, every mistake, every heartbreak, every sleepless night got me here. To this moment. To this version of me.

And I wouldn't trade her for anything.

So if you're reading this and wondering if you can really change, here's my answer: You already are. Every choice you make is a brick in the foundation of the life you're building.

The only question left is, are you building something you actually want to live in?

Your Turn:

Stop waiting for the "right time." Pick one thing today, just one, that moves you closer to the life you've been dreaming about. Then do it like you mean it.

Because you're not here to live someone else's story. You're here to write your own.

The Next Chapter Is Yours to Write:

Step Out of Who You Were Told to Be and Into Who You Really Are

From Me to You

I'm not writing this from the top of the mountain.

I'm writing it from real life.

I've been doing inner work for over twenty years. Therapy. Energy work. Nervous system work. Mindfulness Practices, Awareness practices. All of it. And I still feel my throat tighten when I speak from my heart sometimes. My hands still get a little shaky when I'm about to do something outside my comfort zone. That never changes, it just moves as you grow into a different version of yourself.

So if you're waiting for the day when none of this ever shows up again, let me save you some time:

That day doesn't come.

And that doesn't mean you're failing.

What *does* change is this:
I notice it now, while it's happening.

Not hours later.
Not after I've already overridden myself.

In the moment.

That awareness gives me something I didn't have before.

A choice.

Here's the part most people miss:

When you make a different choice in that moment, even a small one, you're not just "being brave" or "doing the work."

You're building a new neuropathway.

Your brain is literally learning a new route.

And it doesn't care how graceful you were.
It only cares that you did something *different*.

Pause instead of react.
Stay instead of collapse.
Say less instead of over-explaining.

That's how new wiring forms.

But here's the real talk part:

This is a long game.

Those old patterns didn't come from nowhere. They were practiced for years, sometimes decades. So yeah, they're going to show up again. And again. And again. Until they don't!

That doesn't mean the new way isn't working.

It means repetition matters.

Every time you choose differently, the new pathway gets a little stronger.
Every time you interrupt the old move, it loses some ground.

And one day, usually without any big announcement, you realize something strange: You can't remember the last time you reacted the old way, or thought in an old way.

Not because you're trying not to.
Not because you're managing yourself.

It just... doesn't happen anymore.

That's when you know the change is real.

Not because you thought your way there.
But because the new pathway is now deeper than the old one.

That's when everything shifts.

I still catch myself sometimes.

I still choose again.

But I don't panic about it anymore, because I understand the process. I also know that I will continue to expand into the most amazing version of myself. Continuing to grow and love in ways I never thought possible.

Awareness.
Choice.
Repetition.
Patience.

That's how the nervous system learns safety.
That's how patterns dissolve instead of being forced away.

So if you're reading this and thinking, *I know exactly what she's talking about*, good.

You're not behind.
You're not broken.
And you're not late.

You're building something that lasts.

And once the new wiring takes hold, life doesn't feel like such a fight anymore. You get to a place where external things no longer matter as much because inside you have found a love that can't come from another.

You have found peace, and this is when things begin to come to you naturally!

QR CODE INVITE TEXT

If you're ready to stop living someone else's story and start building your own, scan this code. You'll get instant access to tools, trainings, and real conversations that will push you out of autopilot and into a life you want to live.

Scan me!

NOTES

NOTES

NOTES

NOTES

NOTES

NOTES

NOTES

NOTES

NOTES

www.ingramcontent.com/pod-product-compliance
Lightning Source LLC
LaVergne TN
LVHW010700110826
845149LV00014B/3182